The **7** Habits of

Highly Successful

Financial Planners

How to really matter in the lives of your clients

Paul D. Armson

"Essential reading for all Advisers who truly aspire to be the best in their field and who wish to deliver a world class service proposition"
Alan Smith
CEO, Capital Asset Management, London

First published in Great Britain in 2016
by Inspiring Advisers Limited

Dedication

To Mum

For helping me find my 'Why'

Introduction

Why YOU? Why ME? Why NOW?

If ever there was a time to make a difference in the lives of your clients with a compelling, high value financial advice service, that time is right now.

Consumers throughout the Western world are starting to realise that the old fashioned 'commission based' financial services world is bust.

Commissions are becoming more and more transparent - or are being banned altogether. Advisers are being forced to charge fees, and those fees will undoubtedly become more and more explicit over the next few years.

It's just a matter of time before clients start to ask, *"So, what, exactly, are you doing for your fees?"*

The consumer press will continue to hammer all involved in financial services, and they will turn their attention to focus on 'rip off fees'. A recent article in the personal finance section of the Financial Times said that 'many 'investment focused advisers' are charging 'Picasso prices for painting by numbers''. This is just the start.

NOW is the time to use this to your advantage and differentiate yourself from the rest by delivering the WOW factor - by making a difference in your clients' lives.

It's time to deliver a service worth paying for; a service that knocks clients' socks off; a service that clients actually want.

What worked in the past definitely won't work in the future! It's time to WOW your clients like never before.

This book will show you how.

Why is this book relevant to you?

You've invested in this book, so I'm guessing that you want to stay ahead of the game as a Financial Adviser - you want to deliver better outcomes for your clients.

Either way, I'm guessing you want the best for your clients. You want to deliver REAL benefits. I'm also guessing that you want the best for yourself too! YOU want more money, more freedom, more choices. You want more peace of mind and more control over your future. You want the best for yourself and your family. And so you should.

The problem facing most financial advisers is this: traditional financial advice won't work anymore. Not for much longer anyway.

If you want to succeed and prosper in the years ahead, you'll need to set about breaking old habits.

As you'll see, those old habits are not your fault. Most have been 'inflicted' on you by the Financial Services Industry.

And the good news is, you've taken the first step in breaking those habits.

Why should you listen to me?

You might be thinking *"Who the heck are you?"* And *"What gives YOU the right to tell me how to improve my business or my client service?"*

That's a good question.

After all, I started out in life as an Apprentice Carpenter at the age of 16! So why the heck should you listen to me!!

I stopped being a Carpenter at the age of 19. That's when I became a trainee Quantity Surveyor. Because I'd noticed they all had Company Cars!

But then I saw this ad, the headline read:

> "Are you of above average intelligence,
> and wish to earn a six-figure income
> within 3 - 5 years?"

I admit it. I wasn't too sure about the first part of this headline, but I was damned sure about the second part! So I plucked up courage and I made the call.

I got an interview. That's when I 'fell' into the job as a Financial Adviser at the tender age of 22.

By the age of 30 I'd discovered a way of communicating and delivering financial planning that consistently knocked clients socks off. So much so, clients said: *"Why don't ALL financial advisers do what you do?"*

This process - which I now call my **'Lifestyle Financial Planning' Seven Step Success System** - enabled me to consistently enjoy a high six figure income - and to semi-retire at the age of 45 to start sailing my million pound ocean going sailing yacht, *'Spellbound'*, around the world.

Not bad for a council house lad.

But I don't state any of this to impress you. I state this to impress ON you the power of what is contained in the following pages.

For the last 7 years, when I've not been sailing, I've been teaching other Advisers my **'Inspired Adviser 'Lifestyle Financial Planning' Seven Step Success System'** and in the process helped several hundred Financial Advisers to create, promote and deliver a joined up, highly profitable client service proposition that changes lives. It could do the same for you too.

An opportunity to learn from the BEST...

Because of the success of 'Inspiring Advisers' and my 'Seven Step Success System', I'm truly honoured that the '7 Habits' explained in this book are not just based on my own observations and experiences, but also on those of some of the most successful, most effective financial planners in the UK today with whom I have had the pleasure of working. All are members of the amazing Inspiring Advisers community.

A few names worthy of mention and to whom I send my sincere thanks for their friendship and guidance in preparing this book are: Alan Smith of Capital Asset Management, London; Steve Martin, Smart Financial Planning, Cheshire; Graham Ponting, Clearwater Wealth Management, High Wycombe; Ruth Sturkey, The Red House, London; Damien Rylett, Brunel Capital Partners, Bristol; Nick Taylor of Lonsdale Financial Consulting, Tunbridge Wells; Richard Macmillan and Ian Robinson at Forbes Lawson, Aberdeen; Iain Wishart, Wishart Wealth Management, Edinburgh; all are believers in delivering proper financial planning to every single client.

There are now many more, too numerous to mention, thanks to the growing community of inspiring advisers.

Thank you all for your inspiration and commitment to the cause.

Let's get started on the first chapter, in which I need to give you just a little background.

You'll see why…

Chapter One

It happened on a Thursday...

It was a Thursday, and my Dad was hard at work as a welder.

Suddenly, the Foreman in the factory rushed over, tapped him on the shoulder and said *"Derrick! You'd better get home fast! Something's happened to Mary!"*

He dropped everything. He raced out of the factory and into his car.

By the time my Dad had raced the three miles to get home, his wife - my Mum - was dead.

Gone.

She was 59.

My Mum was the first person who mattered in my life to die. It knocked me for six.

But my grief was nothing compared to my Dad's.

You see, losing my Mum was not in his plan.

Here's the sad part...

My Dad had a great work ethic. And when he wasn't working extra shifts at the factory, he'd always be doing odd jobs for other people to earn extra money. He'd cut people's hedges, he'd cut lawns, he'd paint houses. All so he could earn extra money to give us a better life.

For this reason, I didn't see too much of my Dad when I was growing up.

And neither did my Mum.

I think my Mum was quite lonely really. She missed my Dad. He was always working. She knew, though, that he was out there, doing it for us.

But, one day - I must have been about fourteen at the time - something happened between my Mum and my Dad that I'll never forget.

Dad had just got back from the factory. He'd quickly changed clothes - out of his dirty boiler suit and into his gardening clothes - and he was on his way out of the door to do yet another odd job.

With a disappointed look on her face, Mum looked at my Dad and said: *"So.., what time will you be back for your tea, Derrick?"*

I think the *"So.."* gave away how she was feeling.

My Dad, sensing my Mum was a little angry, said *"I'm doing this for us Mary! I'm doing this for us! One day, when I've retired, we'll have plenty of time to spend together, but right now, I have to go to work!"* And off he went.

No, I'll never forget that moment.

You see, they never did get their *"One day…"*

And now, nearly 30 years later, my Dad still misses my Mum.

In fact, he lives his life now, still full of regret.

He lives a life full of *"If only....?"*

"If only I'd spent more time with your Mum" he says, *"If only I'd been there for her"*, *"She loved her flowers, if only I'd bought her more flowers"*, *"If only..."*, *"If only..."*

But it's too late.

Only the other day, we were talking about old times and he said to me, *"Do you remember when you were little, how you said "Daddy, please will you play with me... please?" and I said "Sorry, but I've got to go to work". Do you remember that?"*

Then, with a tear in his eye, he said: *"I wished I'd played with you more often... I wish I'd taken you to watch the football, to see the Wolves play... I wish I'd gone fishing with you like you wanted?"*

Ouch! That hurt.

But he never did - because he was always working. But always for the right reasons you understand. He was living his life the best way he knew how.

I'm proud of my Dad.

Why am I telling you this?

Let me explain.

I'd fallen into financial services and became a financial adviser eight years before my Mum died. It was the eighties - 'Thatchers Britain'! And there I was, working my butt off to earn my six figure income! I was working just as hard as my Dad!

But Mum's death… it was MY wake up call.

Mum's death made me have a long hard look in the mirror. I suddenly realised - back then - that I was now working all the time! I was running around like an idiot. I was the guy who wasn't spending enough time with his family! I was now the busy fool!

Suddenly it dawned on me: I was making exactly the same mistake as my Dad! Different financial results maybe, but I was following in his footsteps - and I was making exactly the same mistake!

I was always, busy, busy, busy. Doing it, doing it, doing it!

That's when I decided, looking in that mirror: NO MORE.

That's when I decided NEVER to work another evening or weekend, ever!

That's when I woke up. That's when I got the message!

My Mum's death woke me up to the one Universal truth:

'Life's not a rehearsal!'

Have you noticed? The older you get the more it feels like time is really speeding up? It's scary. We only have so long on this beautiful planet, we have to make the most of every minute. We have to make sure we do the things we want to do in the small amount of time we've got left!

That's when I decided to be lazier and crazier than I've ever been before!

That's when I decided to start booking time off, *before* I booked time on.

That's when I decided to take time out. To climb more mountains. To sail more seas.

But something more important happened....

Chapter Two

My 'penny dropping moment'...

My life as a Financial Adviser was about to change.

This was my 'penny dropping moment'.

This is the reason why I'm letting you know about my Mum, and my Dad...

Here's how it happened.

A few weeks after my Mum died, I had my first appointment with a prospective new client.

Suddenly, in that meeting, I found my purpose! I found my 'WHY'. I found my reason for being a Financial Adviser.

I've always been good at 'fact-finding' - it was drilled into me by Norman Evans. Norman was my manager in my first job as a financial adviser.

"Be really interested!" he'd say. *"Listen!"* *"Find out where your prospect is in their life; how did they get to where they are now; what's their story? And find out! Where do they want to get to in the future? What sort of life have they got now and what sort of life do they want? Find out!"* he'd say.

So there I am, doing a great fact find, having a really engaging meeting with this lovely couple, Bob & Sandra. They were approaching retirement, and I was asking them what plans they had for their future.

Bob said: *"Well, one day we'd like to do go trekking in New Zealand, and one day we'd like to climb Machu Picchu ...and, you know what Paul, we've both talked about learning to sail and one day buying a boat...."*

"Yes," Sandra added *"...and one day we'd like to cruise the whole Mediterranean!"*

Suddenly, without thinking, I blurted out: *"What was that you both said?"*

They looked at me, somewhat surprised.

"What was that you just said?" I exclaimed!

"ONE DAY...?!?!" I said…

"WHAT MAKES YOU THINK THERE WILL BE A 'ONE DAY'?!" I said, almost slamming the table.

To this day I'm not sure what caused me to be so emotional, but in that meeting, spurred on by the loss of my dear old Mum, something made me challenge them.

"What do you mean by ONE DAY?!" I said. *"Why not do these things now? Why not book these things now, before it's too late?! Life's not a rehearsal, why not do it NOW?!!!"*

It went quiet.

He looked at her. She looked at him.

Had I blown it?

They looked at each other again, in silence.

I apologised for my outburst.

I thought I'd better explain, about the loss of my Mum, and how I'd already noticed that my Dad was now living a life of terrible regret.

I shared with them how I remembered my Dad always saying to my Mum "One day…."

But, for my Mum and my Dad, there was never going to be a 'One day'!

I explained that my Dad would give ANYTHING to be in their position. They had each other. Better still, they had money. They had choices. They had time.

Sadly, my Dad had no money - and no Mary.

They were moved.

That's when they said: "You know what Paul? ….You're absolutely RIGHT!"

Then they admitted they had been going through life always putting things off, working too hard, not spending enough time together. Always saying 'One day…!'

They confessed: *"It's crazy, ...we've been acting like we have forever! But we don't!"*

Then I had turned up. They said it really did seem like I was there for a reason... to 'give them a good shake'!

These 'perfect clients' then looked at me and said *"But, Paul, it's all very well saying 'do it now', but really... can we afford to do these things now?!"*

Luckily, I'd just invested in some comprehensive cashflow modelling financial planning software. That software would eventually change my world - and my income! It would give me the all important answers to this question!

I said *"Leave it with me. I'll see you in a week!"*

After going through all their financial information with a fine tooth comb, and after crunching all the numbers with my new software, the eventual answer for Bob and Sandra, was *"Yes! You can do all these things now* - and, even on very prudent planning assumptions, you'll NEVER run out of money!"

As you can imagine, this lovely couple... they were absolutely thrilled!

It changed Bob and Sandra's life.

They both quit their stressful jobs, and they got on with the business of living life to the full. Because now they knew they could!

But something really important had happened in that first meeting.

Something so incredibly important....

The penny had dropped WITH ME!

Suddenly, I realised that I had engaged with these clients in a completely different way. And they had connected with me differently too! Without at first realising it, my focus had totally changed.

Here's why: I hadn't even talked about their financial products, which was the original purpose of the meeting.

Instead, I'd connected with them about something they could not deny; the ONE undeniable fact that NOBODY can deny:

LIFE IS NOT A REHEARSAL!

These clients knew, deep down, that life is NOT a rehearsal. They knew that their precious time IS slipping away!

Just like you, reading this, YOU know this to be true.

And, deep down, EVERY SINGLE ONE OF YOUR CLIENTS KNOW THIS TO BE TRUE.

Life is NOT a rehearsal. Precious time IS slipping away!

Suddenly, as if by magic, my service proposition changed.

Suddenly, it wasn't about their money anymore or their need for a financial product. I felt like I was no longer on the opposite side to them trying to sell them something.

Instead, I'd made it absolutely clear! I was on THEIR side. I was interested in THEM and what THEY wanted to do in the time they'd got left! It was me and them, facing up to the ONE undeniable truth! It was me and them together; me helping them, inspiring them, cajoling them, reminding them about this thing called 'old age and death' - and the inevitable: that time when you become 'too old to have FUN!' - and then you're dead.

Here's the thing. They could FEEL that my interest was in them, NOT THEIR MONEY.

That's when the penny dropped!

That's when I realised the power and purpose of PROPER financial planning.

That's when I realised, that my job, as a Financial Adviser, was to help clients to GET and KEEP the life they want. To inspire them to do the things that inspire *them and* to do the things *they* want to do, before it's too late. It was my job to help clients identify, achieve and maintain their desired lifestyle - WHATEVER HAPPENS. That was my job.

And, if you're a Financial Adviser, I believe it's your job too!

Clients don't really want financial products, or investments. Never have. And never will.

They want the peace of mind and security of knowing where they're heading financially, and knowing what they need to do to secure their desired lifestyle. That's the only thing that clients want: Lifestyle. It's what they've worked hard for. And it's the one thing they want to keep.

Lifestyle is different for everybody, of course! Some have a big lifestyle. Some have a little lifestyle. Some have a lifestyle that includes gifting to good causes, or perhaps leaving a legacy. But, whichever way you look at it, it's all about lifestyle.

My job, therefore, is to help clients understand *'how much is ENOUGH?':* to help them understand their Number - the amount they need to keep living the life they want.

Once I've helped them to understand their Number - through proper financial planning - my job is then to help them accumulate it, manage it, protect it, and most importantly, ENJOY IT! Before it's too late!

Simple formulae: Big lifestyle = big Number. Little lifestyle = little Number.

What we do, as Financial Advisers, has little or nothing to do with financial products. They are just *'tools in the bag'*, used - when required - to get the job done. Sometimes clients don't need any 'tools' - but that doesn't take away the immense value of an incredible 'PROPER financial planning' service.

These are the realisations I started to come to in the early Nineties.

That's when I decided, there and then, to deliver just ONE service - to ALL clients.

That service was *'Lifestyle' Financial Planning: helping clients to identify, achieve and maintain their desired lifestyle - whatever happens.*

"That's what I do for people!" - the penny had dropped!

It made me feel good. Better still, it made clients feel great too!

Armed with the right tools and the right mindset, I realised I could help ANY client, ANYWHERE.

More important, from that moment forward, my confidence increased. I became more congruent, more believable. I knew exactly what EVERY client wanted: to live a great life in the time they've got left! And, through the delivery of 'Lifestyle' Financial Planning, I knew I could help them get it.

I also started to realise that I was in charge. It was my life!

So I stopped wasting my time seeing people who I couldn't really help or who would never be profitable clients. I stopped being a busy fool!

With my 'alternative' financial advice service, I realised I could decide who I took on as a client. It was ME who decided who I spent MY precious time with.

All I had to do was decide which clients I wanted in my life!

When I approached new prospective clients - the type I wanted in my life - I realised that in order to differentiate myself from the 'rest', I had to introduce myself and my 'alternative' service in a compelling way.

(By the way, all this is easy, when you know how. And this is what I now teach others).

So, I got good at communicating and delivering 'Lifestyle Financial Planning'. I got really good.

This enabled me to enjoy a high six-figure income for many years and enabled me to semi-retire, aged 45, to start sailing my ocean going sailing yacht, *'Spellbound'*, around the world. Yep! Life is too short. You have to walk your talk.

And that's the sort of thing you can do when you get good at communicating and delivering Lifestyle Financial Planning. In fact, you must practice what you preach.

Remember, YOU have every right to have a great lifestyle. In fact, when you help your clients get what they want out of life with Lifestyle Financial Planning they will give you their blessing to do the same.

So, before we move on to the 7 Habits… a quick question:

Why did you join Financial Services?

Like me, did you fall into it? Or did you CHOOSE to be a Financial Adviser?

If you became a Financial Adviser for the money, how's it worked out? Be honest.

Are you still in love with your job? Are you passionate about what you bring to the table? Do you feel really REALLY confident about your future and how you add value to client's lives?

Are you easily able to communicate your client service proposition?

Does it knock clients' socks off?

More important, can you actually deliver a COMPELLING service proposition, time and time again, year after year, so clients say, *"WOW!!! Why don't all Financial Advisers do this?!"*

Can you easily justify your fees, so clients would happily pay you MORE for the benefits that you deliver?

Can you easily get more of the RIGHT type of clients?

You see, these things happen when you cultivate the right habits.

Let's take a look then, at the **SEVEN HABITS OF HIGHLY SUCCESSFUL FINANCIAL PLANNERS**.

These are based on my own experience and those of other successful Planners who I have had the pleasure - and honour - of helping achieve fantastic results with Lifestyle Financial Planning.

Chapter Three

Success Habit No. 1

Connect with clients about the ONE thing they want to keep

Unwittingly, with a little help from the 'Industry' many of us Advisers have fallen into bad habits. We've traditionally focused our service on all the wrong things. And, for years and years, it's worked. We got away with it.

We 'got away with it' for one reason and one reason only: because the way in which most of us were paid was - let's be honest - less than transparent. It was through 'smoke & mirrors': through commission, or more recently, through less than transparent 'fees'. Even now, many Advisers are relying on a 1% 'fee' model which, in many cases, is nothing more than commission in disguise. And, until recently, much of this has been disguised by fund rebates and the like.

Quite simply, in the past, clients didn't really know how, or how much they were paying for financial advice. But now that's all changing.

Let's cut to the chase....

Clients don't really want financial products. They never have and never will. But, sadly, it's what they've come to expect us Advisers to talk about. And it's boring. And because of vested interests, the 'Industry', (including the Regulators) continue to keep the focus on products and investments.

Now why might that be, I wonder?

Because this is where the 'Industry' makes its money! I'd go as far as saying that the 'Industry' doesn't care about your clients. It only cares about itself.

But here lies YOUR OPPORTUNITY.

All you need to do is this: adopt Success Habit No. 1!

Do the exact opposite of what everyone else is doing.

Instead of focusing your service on products and investments, do the complete opposite.

Do what the most successful Financial Planners do: **focus on your clients, not their money.**

Do this right, and clients will then trust you with ALL of their money!

What do clients really want?

Well, they don't want financial products, that's for sure. And they don't want mind numbingly boring meetings with an Adviser about the pros and cons of this product over that product, or dull, boring 'annual review' meetings.

Most don't care about technical minutiae, or about basis points and product options. They don't really care about performance. (TIP: If you've got clients who do focus on investment performance then it's time to sack those clients! That is, if you want a peaceful life!)

If clients appear interested when Advisers go on and on and on about product features or investment market analysis or product charges - here's some news:

They are NOT interested.

Here's what's happening…. they are just being polite! And, in the past, it was easy for clients to be polite - because they didn't realise how much they were paying in fees!

And, sorry to break this to you, but clients don't really care about your qualifications either. Or about you being 'independent' and 'unbiased'; about you being 'experienced' and 'trustworthy'.

These are NOT things that clients <u>want</u>. Not at all.

These are things they EXPECT!

Think about it! Clients don't go to their Doctor, because he's qualified and because he always gives them the 'right medicine'.

They expect him to!

Yet most Advisers focus on exactly these things - mere expectations. That's after they've bored their clients to tears with money laundering regulations and compliance disclosures!

No, a meeting with a Financial Adviser is not the sexiest thing in the world!

But what if YOU did the opposite?

What if you changed the way you communicated your service?

What if YOU got re-inspired about the work you do so that clients WANTED to do business with you and you only. And what if they were KEEN to pay you well for it - and were EXCITED to refer you to their friends?

What if?

Here's the key...

Doing the opposite means giving clients what THEY want - not what the Financial 'Industry' wants.

So, what do clients want?

What do they REALLY want?

Deep down, every good Adviser knows that clients want the BIG things. They want the BENEFITS. They want peace of mind, financial security, and financial independence. That's more like it, don't you think?

But how do you communicate that? How do you promote that as the outcome of your service? It's all a bit woolly. Sounds nice. But what does *peace of mind* or *financial security* really mean?

I think there is something more. There's something more important that clients want. In fact, I'd go as far as saying that there is only ONE thing that clients REALLY want.

So, wouldn't it make sense to focus your service on communicating and delivering exactly that? Wouldn't it make sense to focus your service on that ONE THING?

Forgive me for sounding perhaps a tad shallow, but, when you think about it, there's only ONE thing clients want; there's ONE thing they bust a gut for.

There's only ONE thing for which they work all the hours the Universe sends.

There's only ONE thing that keeps them awake at night.

There's only ONE thing they want to be sure of.

And there's only ONE thing they want to keep.

In fact, this ONE THING is so important it is the very thing that determines whether 'Financial Security', 'Financial Independence' and 'Financial Peace of Mind' will ever be achieved!

It's so important it determines whether these things can ever be obtained!

Let me prove it to you.

Right now, you (and every single one of your clients) could be totally financially independent, right now.

Yes. You could have total financial security and complete peace of mind - right now.

All you've got to do is this:

Step 1. Sell your car and / or sell your house,

Step 2. Take whatever money you are left with, and go here…

…NEPAL.

Take a cheap flight to Kathmandu, then a short internal flight into Lukla Airport, and then start trekking North. You'll soon come to one of many wonderful little villages, all nestled in a beautiful valley.

Here you can buy yourself a little shack - for next to nothing. Do that, and in that village, you will be the richest person around.

That's all you've got to do… and you've got it…

Total financial independence!

You need never worry about money ever again. Sorted.

Now, you might have to walk a few miles for your water, or go gather wood for your fire, - but you will be financially secure for the rest of your life. And, of course, in the mountains, it's a great place to find REAL peace of mind!

"Ah, but…!" I hear you say… *"What about my BMW? And what about my yacht? And what about my Bang & Olufsen music system? What about the nice things in life?"*

Suddenly it doesn't seem quite so appealing.

So, all of a sudden, what was easily achievable - *'Financial Independence'* - is now no longer possible.

For one reason and one reason only…

LIFESTYLE!

Think about it. It's the only thing that anybody wants! And it's the only thing they want to keep (apart from their health).

So, what if you could make that ONE thing the very focus of your service?

What if all your focus, energy and communication was directed towards understanding and helping clients achieve their DESIRED lifestyle?

That ONE thing, LIFESTYLE - the ONLY thing that clients want - is the very thing you should focus your service on.

It's THE thing the BEST financial planners focus on. They've made it a HABIT.

The focus of their service is not about their client's investments! It's about helping clients identify, achieve and maintain their desired lifestyle without risk of running out of money - or dying with too much. It's about helping clients GET and KEEP a great life!

Personally, that's what I've been focusing on and delivering for years. That's why I call it: 'Lifestyle' Financial Planning!

It's Financial Planning with an end in mind.

The 'end' is helping clients to get and KEEP a great life!

It's NOT about being top quartile! Or clever planning to save a few quid in tax. None of that matters in comparison.

Lifestyle is what people work hard to achieve. Lifestyle is what people want to enjoy. Lifestyle is what people want to maintain and improve.

Of course, 'Lifestyle' is different for everybody, and that's what makes our job interesting!

Lifestyle could be sailing a yacht around the world, or simply being able to live 'a comfortable life' or being able to gift to good causes or perhaps create a foundation - something that lives on after they're gone.

Our job then is about understanding clients and then helping them identify, achieve and maintain their desired lifestyle, so they end up with a life worth living. A life well lived. That is what we should be doing for people.

The solution:

Make it a habit! Understand your clients current and future desired lifestyle. Make it the focus of your service. How? By asking the right questions. By listening. By being more interested in your clients than their money.

But how do we do that?

Easy.

Be interested in them and their story.

We've all got a story. You've got a story. I've got a story. Every single one of your clients has a story. But no-one is really interested in our story, because, sadly, the human condition is to be only interested in ourselves.

However, this provides you with an incredible opportunity.

Which brings me to Success Habit No. 2…

Chapter Four

Success Habit No. 2

Be interested. Be with the one you're with.

Be honest. How often do you have a meeting with a client and most of the time, your head is busy thinking about what to say next? Do you REALLY listen? Do you really find out about THEM? About what THEY want? Do you really connect?

Or, do you have that meeting with the intention of focusing on financial products and investments?

If we haven't got structure in our first meeting process (the most important meeting of all - the one in which trust is created - or destroyed), if we haven't got a 'client focused' process, a track on which to run, if we don't know what comes next, then our head is going to be very busy - and not always where it should be. And it will show.

Sadly, in recent years, as Advisers have become more and more qualified, the focus has been well and truly on technical skills. Whilst such skills are important, they are not the MOST important. What's missing for many are the all important 'soft skills'.

Ever noticed? It seems many Advisers would rather talk about the in-depth technical minutiae of retirement products or investments rather than ask clients some meaningful questions about what really matters to them - and then just shut up and listen to the answers!

But you don't have to be like most Advisers.

What if you did connect with clients, in that precious moment?

What if you could 'relax' in that meeting? And become more present?

That's when the magic happens!

Every client we meet provides a unique opportunity to connect with another human being. And that's special.

Let's face it, on a day-to-day basis, clients encounter pretty meaningless, shallow, uncaring 'relationships' with countless institutions - with staff at banks, utilities, shops, stores, other professionals, colleagues - and friends even. No-one is REALLY interested in them. Almost everyone they encounter is too busy 'just doing their job' and just going through life, looking after 'No.1'.

Nobody out there is REALLY interested in your client. In THEM, in THEIR story. There are a lot of people interested in their money, yes. But not in them, not in their story.

Nobody.

And then... you show up!

Sorry to go a bit deep here, but consider this: Every client that you meet with, whether they be a new or existing client, deep down is lonely. They're insecure. You, reading this, deep down, are lonely. Go on. Admit it.

You're insecure, and you know it. We all are - if we are brave enough to admit it. It comes with being human. This mind-made sense of self that we've each created is very fragile.

So, knowing this, why not use it to your advantage! In a good way!

CONNECT!

BE with your clients. Be interested. Be really, REALLY interested, in them and in their story. They will love you for it!

In other words, be interested in… their LIFESTYLE.

Where are they now in their life?

How did they get to where they are now?

What sort of trials and tribulations have they been through? What successes have they had, and what failures?

And then, when you've built rapport by being interested in their past….

Where do they want to get to in the future?

What sort of lifestyle have they got now, and more important, what type of lifestyle do they want to have in the future.

What do they want to do before it's too late and they're 'too old to enjoy themselves' or they're dead in a box.

What is their STORY? Remember, we all have a story. You've got one, I've got one. Be interested in THEIR story.

That's how we build trust, by being genuinely interested in our client - a fellow human being - with fears and doubts and wants and needs and dreams and goals.

Once uncovered, our job, is to help those dreams come true, to help clients live the life they want, to help them get what they want out of life, before it's too late.

When we make it a HABIT of taking the focus OFF the money, and instead focusing on our client, finding out what THEY want out of life - in particular, their LIFESTYLE - clients can then see that our interest is in them, not their money. They realise that we are interested in helping THEM get what THEY want.

Then, as if by magic, without you trying to sell anything, they trust you with ALL their money.

But first, you've got to connect.

Need help? Fancy making this a HABIT?

If this has resonated with you, or you need help communicating this to clients, if you'd like to improve your 'soft skills', your 'fact-finding' skills, if you'd like to hold more enjoyable and satisfying client meetings where you can discover what your clients really want and then go on to communicate your service in a compelling way, then you might like to take a look at 'Trust Builder - the Digging Deeper Fact Finding System'. It's part of my 'Seven Step 'Lifestyle Financial Planning' Success System'. In this I share 30 years experience of holding client-focused meetings which keep the focus where it belongs by avoiding 'The Transaction Trap', thereby creating more trust and eventually justifying much bigger fees. **You can take a 30 day no risk trial by going here.**

Or go to: www.FPsuccesssystem.co.uk

Chapter Five

Success Habit No. 3

Tell the Truth... About Money.

Most Financial Advisers don't tell the truth about money. They are not lying. They just don't tell the truth. Let me explain.

Years ago I realised that it was my job - my RESPONSIBILITY - to tell clients what I call: *'The Truth About Money'*.

The 'Truth About Money' is NOT this fund is better than that fund; or this pension is better than that pension; or this product provider is better than that product provider. That is just 'Industry' noise. None of which really matters.

Sadly, however, that's where most financial advisers spend their time. It's become a bad habit. They put way too much focus on stuff that doesn't really matter. Besides, none of it revolves around the <u>truth</u>.

All this 'product stuff' tends to revolve around 'an opinion'. It could be based on great research or analysis, but 'Sod's Law' says it will be wrong. With hindsight there will always be something better you could have done. (Pick a fund today and in a years time you'll probably have wished you'd picked a different fund.) So, focusing your service on things you can't control, like investments, is a recipe for disaster. And, it ain't telling the <u>truth</u>.

The 'Truth About Money' though... is far bigger than that.

The Truth About Money changes clients lives.

The Truth About Money revolves around ONE undeniable FACT.

It's a fact that NO ONE can argue with:

- **that Life is Not A Rehearsal!**

- **that precious time is slipping away!**

- **that the older you get the faster time seems to go...**

...and then, sooner than you imagined, you can't do 'stuff' anymore! Your knees have gone, your hips have gone, you're worn out, you're knackered! Then you're in a wheelchair - and then... you're dead.

This, is an undeniable FACT.

You can't argue with it. Nor can any one of your clients.

So, wouldn't it be better to focus your service on FACT rather than fiction? Focus your service on the FACT that Life is not a rehearsal; that precious time IS slipping away. Because this enables you to have far deeper, more meaningful conversations with clients and demonstrate that you are interested in them more than you are their money. It also brings a sense of urgency to financial planning!

The 'Truth about Money' is therefore:

- What do you want to achieve between now and the day you die?
- When can you stop doing what you no longer enjoy?
- When can you start doing more of the things you love?
- How much do you need to sell your business for in order to live the life you want without fear of ever running out of money, whatever happens?
- What gives your life meaning? What gives your life purpose?
- What needs to happen to secure your family's future so they never worry about running out of money, whatever happens?

And it's about answering the BIGGEST question of all for clients…

• HOW MUCH IS ENOUGH?

How much do YOU need to enable you to live the life you want without fear of running out of money?

By the way, with this question… I'm talking to you!

How much do YOU need?

Is it £1 million? £2 million? £5 million? £20 million?

What is <u>your</u> NUMBER?

Most Financial Advisers I've met don't even know their OWN Number! So, naturally, they fail to answer these questions for clients. They fail to tell the 'Truth'.

But never mind 'most' Advisers.

What if YOU did?

What if you made it a habit?

What if you did what the BEST 'Lifestyle Financial Planners' do?

What if YOU focused <u>your</u> service on asking and answering those BIG questions?

What if you dedicated your service to telling clients the real *'Truth About Money'*?

What if you focused your service on helping clients realise that it's NOT about the cheapest ISA or the best performing fund?

Let me tell you what would happen, from my own personal experience, and from my experience of having coached some of the BEST Lifestyle Financial Planners:

- You would change clients lives.

- You would earn 3 - 5 times what you are earning right now, <u>at least</u>.

- You would change your own life, immeasurably.

- You would feel fantastic about the work you do.

- You would have a real purpose. A WHY.

- You would become more believable. More inspiring. More referable.

- You would conveniently have LESS clients who will happily pay you MORE money.

- You'd spend less time on things that don't matter and more time on things that do.

- You'd get to live the life YOU want. (This is important. You have to lead by example.)

So, if you can engage with clients about the *'Truth About Money'*, if you can subtly (or when necessary ABRUPTLY!) remind clients that Life Is Not A Rehearsal and that it's your job to help clients live the life they want, **clients will find it AMAZING!** Certainly compared to meaningless 'Industry' drivel about products and features.

Plus, you'll easily differentiate yourself from most other Advisers who just don't get it and only want to focus on products.

You see, if you tell *'the Truth About Money'*, it creates better relationships that always results in you doing MORE financial services business and earning bigger and better, stickier fees - and all without really trying.

Believe me, this stuff works. It worked for me and it can work for you too.

How do you think the BEST Lifestyle Financial Planners are now building great businesses and a great life for themselves and their families, all whilst knocking clients socks off.

FACT: If they can do it, you can do it too.

All you need is the right mindset and the right words used in the right order. And that's what I teach.

If this has resonated with you and you'd like to find out more about communicating this message to clients then all this is covered in my 'Inspired Adviser' Seven Step Success System. It's a convenient online training resource that can help you move your service and your business to the next level in six months or less. You can take a no risk trial by going here.

Or go to: www.FPsuccesssystem.co.uk

Chapter Six

Success Habit No. 4

Keep the focus where it belongs and avoid 'The Transaction Trap'

Even with all the best intentions, when it comes to promoting a financial planning service proposition, there's something really important to understand.

I became aware of it many years ago.

It's this…

...Clients won't understand PROPER financial planning _until_ _they experience it._

Until they experience it, they'll think your service is like every other Adviser's service. i.e. about products. And that's boring, not sexy.

But, of course, it's not unusual for clients to come to you with queries about their products or investments. Remember, they themselves have also been conditioned by the consumer financial press to think about products. Why? Because every newspaper or financial website is full of advertisements making a fortune selling advertising space flogging the latest new funds (the 'Industry' peddling its products).

Or, perhaps clients may come to you concerned by scaremongering articles written by unqualified journalists worrying the masses about financial products.

Here's the thing. If you make the mistake of engaging with a client about products; if you start talking about pensions or investments, you will not only be like every other Adviser out there, but you will quickly fall into what I call '**The Transaction Trap'.**

Falling into the 'The Transaction Trap' can be a habit. But it can be changed.

The Transaction Trap happens when you start a client meeting with talk about financial products, or investments. Perhaps because they raise the subject e.g. "I'm worried about my pension!" etc. Or perhaps YOU do?

In fact, I've identified that one of the most common causes of Advisers falling into the 'Transaction Trap' is because they ask one really stupid question to start a meeting...

They ask: "How can I help you?"

Sounds pretty harmless. But it's a stupid question.

It's too open. You have no control. You will find yourself talking about financial products when you shouldn't be! You'll be like 'most' financial advisers.

Here's what happens. As soon as you get embroiled in a conversation about such matters it's very difficult to steer the conversation towards PROPER financial planning.

If you try, they'll think you are trying to 'up-sell' them. They might even ask "How much does this 'financial planning service' cost?" and then, when they find out, they'll say something like: *"Umm. That's interesting. And I would like that. But, not now, perhaps next year. Right now, can you just fix my pension!"* (Or my ISA, investment, mortgage etc).

So, you might end up doing a financial transaction, but you'll never get round to telling the *Truth About Money*. As a result you will end up 'busy' - with yet another product / transaction based relationship which is probably unprofitable, long term. This may have happened to you a few times already!

Am I right?

Here's how to avoid the Transaction Trap and keep the focus where it belongs:

Make it a habit to wear THREE HATS!

Twenty years ago I realised there were THREE distinct parts to my job:

1) **Lifeplanner** - This is the Hat I wear in the Fact Finding / client discovery meetings, it involves really getting to 'know your client' - their story, their LIFESTYLE requirements now and in the future, their goals and objectives, their fears, their doubts. In other words what

sort of life have they got now and what sort of life do they want to keep! What do they want to do before it's too late! What do they want to do before they are *too old to enjoy themselves!* It's finding out about their story!

2) **Financial Planner** - this is the Hat I wear when I go away to crunch the numbers, looking at ALL their financial arrangements; their existing current and future assets and liabilities; their current and future inflows and outflows, IN PARTICULAR the cost of their current and future desired lifestyle. And then it's putting all this together to identify *'HOW MUCH IS ENOUGH?'*

And of course it's the Hat I wear during the Financial Planning meeting as I engage with clients and deliver the Financial Plan - helping them see what their financial future looks like using Financial Forecasting / cashflow modelling software. This is when clients can see that I have their best interests at heart. It's all about THEM and helping them get and keep the life they want without risk or fear of running out of money, or dying with too much!

3) and lastly, **if necessary**, the THIRD AND LEAST IMPORTANT HAT is the **'boring' Financial Adviser Hat!** This is where I would do any necessary Product Implementation / IFA work. And that part of the job

could be kept as simple, painless and low risk as possible.

I realised that these were THREE really important roles that I fulfilled in delivering a great Lifestyle Financial Planning service.

The only trouble was, all of these important stages of the job were lost! They were wrapped up in my 'Industry' title of 'Financial Adviser'!

I wasn't COMMUNICATING my three hats! I was just going round calling myself a 'Financial Adviser'.

But, people don't trust Financial Advisers!

In fact, back then, I was embarrassed to call myself a 'Financial Adviser!'

So, I made a decision.

I believed I did things differently and I wanted to differentiate myself.

So, I started to communicate the fact that I wear THREE HATS! I started to tell prospective clients that there were

THREE important parts to my job. I would say something along these lines:

First I'd make sure I avoid the 'Transaction Trap' by saying:

"Thanks for seeing me today, Steve. I understand you've been introduced to us by your <Accountant>, <Jim>, is that correct?"

"Can I ask, Steve, what has <Jim> told you about who we are and what we do?"

I then shut up and listen. I'm just giving them an opportunity to speak as soon as possible. I'm not going to get too concerned by what they say, either.

Then I'll say something like: *"Well, Steve, as I say thanks for coming in to see us today. And it's nice to know that <Jim> has told you that we are worth talking to. But, what I'd like to say to you right up front Steve is this, that although <Jim> thinks we're the <bees knees/great/worth talking to etc,> I have to say, right up front, that although we have been of great benefit to many of <Jim's> clients, I can't guarantee, at this stage, whether or not we can be of any interest or benefit to you."*

"So, the purpose of this first meeting is for us to get to know each other a little, I'll be asking you some questions about you, and what you are trying to achieve, and, in the course of our conversation, you also will find out a little more about us and how we operate, so then, in about <an hour> **you'll then be in a position to decide whether or not you want to take it any further with us or not, is that OK with you, Steve?"**

This has completely relaxed the prospect. I've avoided the *Transaction Trap*. I am now in control.

I then say: *"In order to make the best use of our time together, I'm going to be going through my confidential questionnaire. This just helps me to stay on track, and to make sure I ask the right questions in the right order. If, at the end of this meeting, you feel that you don't want to take it any further with us, you can simply have this form back and destroy it.* **Is that OK with you Steve?"**

Steve is now even more relaxed. He can see I'm not trying to sell him anything. More important, he can see I'm not desperate for his business. And, he can walk away if he wants. There's no pressure!

I'm in control.

Then, because I've got his permission, I'll start by going through MY questions, in the order I want to ask them, which, as you've probably guessed, are all about STEVE!!!!

If Steve asks: *"HEY!!! But what about my pension? I've come to talk about my pension!!"*

I'll say something like…

"Steve, we do things differently. I understand you may be interested in <pensions>. Now, whereas most financial advisers will happily talk about and sell you a <pension> so they satisfy your short term needs and so they can earn their fees or commission, we don't do that.

In fact, we believe in doing the complete opposite to most financial advisers. So, today's meeting is NOT about financial products. Today's meeting is about YOU and what YOU want.

In fact, Steve, I believe that until I know about YOU and what YOU want, then I have no right to talk about your money - or tell you what to do with it!

So, the way we do things differently, Steve, is there are three very distinct parts to my job, I effectively wear THREE hats.

The first hat, which is the hat I'm wearing today, is that of 'Lifeplanner'. The Lifeplanner's job is to find out about you and what you want; about where you are in your life, about how you got to where you are in your life, and now, where you are trying to get to in the next 5 years, 10 years, 20 years. In particular, what type of lifestyle do you enjoy now and what kind of lifestyle do you want to enjoy in the future?

In other words, what do you want to achieve in what little time you've got left on this planet? Life's not a rehearsal! Precious time is slipping away! So, what do you want to do before it's too late and you're in a box?

When I know that, I'll then be in a position to put on my 2nd Hat, which is that of a Financial Planner. The Financial Planner's job is to identify ALL of the resources available to you today; ALL of the resources becoming available to you in the future, and - if necessary - all of the resources that might NEED to come available to you in order to provide for the life you want to live. That's called financial planning and it's designed to help you realise, perhaps for the first time, the choices available to you to enable you to live the life you want.

Finally, **IF** that Financial Plan indicates that you MIGHT need a financial product or investment, **IF** it does, THEN *and ONLY THEN will I put on my third and LEAST important hat - which is that of an Independent Financial Adviser where I will then find the right product or investment, from the whole market place, that best suit the needs of your financial plan. This means that any financial recommendation we may make will be based on your REAL needs."*

I would then go through my Confidential 'Fact Find' Questionnaire, asking the right questions in the right order, and use various simple scripts and a powerful no obligation 'risk reversal' technique to easily engage the client in a meaningful conversation about THEM, THEIR LIFE, THEIR FAMILY, their goals and objectives, etc. In other words I would demonstrate my interest was in them, not their money. This builds trust so clients would then tell me EVERYTHING I needed to know. In the process of this 'fact finding' meeting I would also subtly gather information about their existing financial arrangements in order for me to go to the next stage of the process: Financial Planning.

It worked every time.

Got that?

Here's what happened. When I started to break down my job like this it meant I could easily deflect any talk about financial products - so I easily avoided the 'Transaction Trap'.

It meant I was different to most Advisers they'd met before because I wasn't talking about financial products.

You see, when you can confidently say: **"I know that your main concern is [product/pension/investment etc] but the way I see it is until I know about you and what you are trying to achieve I have no right to talk about your money - or tell you what to do with it!"**

Suddenly clients eyes light up. They'd often say to me: *"You mean you are not here to try and sell me something?"*

Correct.

This shows you are confident. You're not desperate for their business, and, in the process, this approach builds massive trust.

So, here's a quick question. Could YOU think of your service in this way?

Could you adopt a new habit, with the help of some simple 'scripts' that explain how you are different to other Advisers?

Could you re-engage EXISTING clients and communicate and deliver a more meaningful, enhanced service proposition that has their REAL needs at heart? Could you do this so existing clients would happily increase and keep paying your fees?

I bet you could.

All you have to do is this: let the penny drop! Feel it in your heart! Understand your true role - of helping clients GET and KEEP the life they want.

Then, you just need to make it a habit! You just need to get good, really good, at delivering your first meeting / fact find / discovery meeting. You need to get good at asking the RIGHT questions in the RIGHT order. You just need to understand and BELIEVE in the 'Truth About Money'. Then you will easily engage clients in proper financial planning - which WILL result in bigger and better fees for you. Promise.

If this 'Three Hats' concept resonates with you, if you think you could adopt it, then I can show you how to deliver the message so clients say, "WOW! Why don't all financial advisers do this?!!!"

All this is covered in my 'Seven Step Success System"
You can find out more and benefit from a <u>30 day No
Risk Trial by going here</u>.

Or go to: <u>www.FPsuccesssystem.co.uk</u>

Chapter Seven

Success Habit No. 5

Help clients see what their financial future looks like

Imagine having clients take 'ownership' of their financial plan?

Imagine a second meeting with a prospective client where you wear your 'Second Hat' to deliver proper financial planning.

Imagine clients 'experiencing' for the first time what PROPER financial planning feels like, so they are not only *WOWed* by your service but also feel confident to make solid, sensible decisions about their future. This results in clients saving more, investing more, protecting more - and paying you more. More important, this results in you securing that client relationship for life - doing more business and making a lot more money in the process.

This is undoubtedly what sets the BEST financial planners apart. They make it a habit to engage clients in the financial planning process.

The best way I've found to do this is by demonstrating what financial planning **feels** like through the effective and proper use of 'client focused' Financial Forecasting Software (also known as Cashflow Modelling software).

Used properly, using prudent assumptions, the right software enables you to show what a clients future looks like in an engaging and thought provoking way. It enables you to have meaningful discussions about the one thing that matters most (their lifestyle). And helps you to tell the *'Truth About Money'* by confidently answering their BIG questions, like **HOW MUCH IS ENOUGH?**

Used properly, you can paint an accurate picture, based on conservative assumptions about whether a client is on course to run out of money, or die with too much.

You can help clients realise that they CAN afford to take that world cruise, buy that yacht or take that redundancy package.

You can help older clients realise they CAN easily afford to keep their heating on in the winter!

You can help couples realise that they can afford to retire now and spend precious time together whilst they are still young enough and fit enough to 'do stuff'. Life's not a rehearsal!

Here's the thing: With cashflow modelling software, used properly, you are differentiating yourself once again by taking the focus OFF products and investments and putting it on the only thing that matters - your client's life! And on helping them get the most out of it.

Without 'selling' you can easily help clients save more and invest more. You can help them understand how much life insurance and critical illness protection they need, and show that they can easily afford it. This gives them the security of KNOWING that YOU are making sure that things are going to be OK, whatever happens.

You can help clients see they can afford to live more, do more and give more! For example, perhaps you could prove to them that they can easily afford to spend another £20,000 a year on travel in the first 10 years of their retirement - while they are still fit enough to do stuff. This can make someone's day!

You can 'de-risk' clients by helping them realise that they are never going to run out of money - so why take unnecessary investment risk? This can take away unnecessary worry and stress and give real peace of mind.

You can help a business owner work out their 'Number' - the amount they need for the rest of their life. You can help them understand how much they need to sell their business for. You can help them understand how much more money they need to make each year to secure their future.

With it you can change client's lives.

Using the THREE HAT concept, Cashflow Modelling software demonstrates and delivers your second Hat: your work as a Financial Planner. It PROVES you do financial planning. Client's then 'get it'. They understand the immense value you bring to the table. And all this without you trying to sell a single financial product!

After delivering to clients a Financial Planning 'experience', if you've used cashflow modelling properly, clients will quickly commit to investing more, saving more, protecting more, etc. so that you can then confidently move your service on to the third stage of the job (your third Hat) which is 'Product / Investment Implementation'. That's the easy part. And you'll now do tons more business without really trying.

Here's the best bit: because your service no longer needs to revolve around investment performance, or being first quartile, or knocking the lights out, you can keep the product implementation piece (your Third Hat) as simple, low risk and painless as possible.

If you would like to understand cashflow modelling, how it works and how to use it with clients with absolute confidence, then I can show you how. My 'Seven Step Success System' includes a whole module on the effective use of cashflow modelling software and will show you how to WOW clients by showing them what their financial future looks like.

It will also show you how to avoid the seven biggest mistakes that other Advisers are making with cashflow modelling. You can take a 30 day no risk trial by going here.

Or go to: www.FPsuccesssystem.co.uk

Chapter Eight

Success Habit No. 6

Keep the 'money stuff' as simple as possible.

OK, you're a Financial Adviser, and you've read this far.

Here's the best bit. And it's why the BEST financial planners are building successful businesses with the minimum of hassle.

If you can get really good at this 'Lifestyle Financial Planning' lark, the 'money stuff' becomes less important.

You will realise that the important stuff is in Hats 1 & 2. That's where your value is.

More important, by now you will have created massive levels of trust because you haven't been trying to sell anything. You have simply been showing how you are committed to helping clients live the life they want. Your focus has become helping clients get what THEY want.

But, you still have to implement financial products where necessary. In fact, using this approach you'll probably have to implement an awful lot more - and much, much bigger transactions. You'll also easily attract clients and huge levels of client assets away from other advisers. Why? Because you'll do something for those clients that they don't!

The good news is this: whereas in the past you might have felt the need to impress clients with your knowledge of investment markets (ahem), or your promises to deliver superior returns (ahem)...

Or perhaps you focused on your 'independence' and your ability to access the whole market..

Or perhaps you often felt under pressure because of the constant requirement to come up with something new; some 'different' type of investment or fund, or some 'special investment' or alternative product, perhaps to justify your fees...

Suddenly, none of that matters anymore!

Phew!

You no longer have to try to 'beat the market', be top quartile, or deliver 'spectacular' returns for clients - better than their friends down the pub are achieving! You don't have to try to impress clients with fancy investments or complicated portfolios that can get you into real trouble and cause you a constant headache.

It's understandable if you once felt that this was necessary - to enable you to justify your service and your fees. But not anymore. (Remember, it wasn't your fault! The 'Industry' made you do it!)

From now on, if you get into the habit of adopting a 'Lifestyle Financial Planning' approach using my techniques, you can keep the recommendations **as simple, painless and risk free as possible**. There's no longer any need to try to shoot the lights out. No longer any need to promise returns that you may not be able to deliver. No need to cause yourself stress.

All you need to do from this point forward is align simple solutions to deliver prudent returns in line with conservative financial planning assumptions. The client's financial plan (based on prudent cashflow modelling) becomes the focus and the only benchmark you care about. Financial products and investments simply become the 'tools in your bag' - used when necessary to get the job done. That's all they are. Tools in the bag. You no longer need to do what other Advisers do: bore clients to death talking about the tools in your bag!

What a relief!

So, if ever you wanted to get a simple more peaceful life this is it. All the 'BS' the Industry talks about won't bother you anymore. Clients will worry you less. They won't panic if markets go up and down. Their focus becomes the long term with you helping them live the life they want. Better still, they won't really care about charges. They won't really care about total expense ratios.

They'll just trust you to do the right thing.

Chapter Nine

Success Habit No. 7

Make ongoing 'Forward Planning Meetings' a pleasure, not a pain.

So many Advisers seem to have a 'client review service' which revolves around half-yearly or yearly meetings discussing and reviewing the progress and performance of a clients' products and investments. Not only is that boring, it's a recipe for disaster! This may have worked in the past, when clients didn't know how much they were paying for your service, but not anymore. Not when clients are starting to learn what financial advice is really costing them.

Consider this: in the past, if clients didn't really know how much they were paying in fees or commissions, then, no matter what service an Adviser offered or delivered - no matter how BAD that service was - even if it was just reviewing their products and investments - they got away with it! Why? Because many clients thought it was 'free'! They didn't know how, or how much they were paying for it.

But that's all changing.

So, that's why many Advisers felt they had to come up with something new every year to try and impress their clients and justify their existence. And, of course, the 'Industry' just loves that! The 'Industry' happily keeps coming up with new funds - and new marketing initiatives - to give Advisers something to talk about with their clients. And the 'financial porn' - the financial trade press - makes a fortune selling advertising space and dubious 'advertorials' promoting those new funds!

And, it worked. Advisers could recommend something new and shift their clients money around and clients were OK with that - because they didn't really know how much this was costing them!

This won't work any more.

FACT: Advisers can't get away with a 'product / investment review' service for much longer.

As the financial advice world moves more and more to transparent fees, if you want to keep those fees then you'll need to deliver a meaningful service, year after year, in exchange for those fees. Fail to do so and clients will stop paying you. It's as simple as that.

Here's the really good news....

This is exactly why 'Lifestyle Financial Planning' makes so much sense! And why the BEST financial planners have such a great future...

Lifestyle Financial Planning delivers an ongoing, demonstratable service that re-engages clients every year - year after year - and delivers to them real benefits as you continue to help them have clarity, peace of mind, financial security and financial independence.

This really is the best bit. And the BEST financial planners will confirm it:

Every year your service can be EXACTLY the same.

Every year 90 - 95% of your meeting can be spent focused on your client; on their life and their lifestyle - and 10% (or less) spent on reviewing the progress of their existing products or investments.

So, the BEST financial planners don't have 'review meetings'. They've made it a habit to have *'Forward Planning Meetings'*.

'Forward Planning Meetings' using my Lifestyle Financial Planning approach become something that clients really look forward to. They become a pleasure - not a pain.

All you have to do is make it a habit to re-engage them in the Financial Planning process, to remind them about the purpose of the meeting (to ensure they are on track to achieve the life they want and maintain their desired lifestyle without running out of money or dying with too much!)

Better still, as this habit gets stronger, you can confidently use the same words and the same processes every year. This means that clients really get to understand what you deliver. So, instead of always meeting with a client and saying something different (about the latest product / portfolio recommendation), instead, you deliver the SAME service, using the SAME words and processes. This means clients get used to your service. They rely on it. They trust you more and more - and are more inclined to refer you to their friends - because they see how consistent you are. They truly BELIEVE in you and the benefits of your service.

So, the key is in making the ongoing service as enjoyable and as client focused as possible. If you would like to find out how to do this then my 'Seven Step Success System' will show you how. You can sign up for a no risk, 30 day trial by <u>going here</u>.

Or go to: <u>www.FPsuccesssystem.co.uk</u>

Chapter Ten

Success Habit 'Extra Bonus'

Satisfaction Guaranteed: Make it a Habit to Explain & Deliver your service in a compelling way.

I've kept this one till last on purpose. Because this is what will make or break you in the years ahead.

Sorry to keep hitting you over the head with it, but traditional financial advice is dead. Over the next few years more and more clients will abandon their financial adviser and take care of their own finances on the internet. Do It

Yourself options for clients will become sexier and sexier. Robo-Advice is coming, whether you like it or not. Those clients that do stick with their Adviser for 'financial advice' will eventually put them under increasing pressure to reduce their fees.

So, if you go out into the world promoting yourself as a 'Financial Adviser' or 'Investment Adviser' or 'Wealth Manager' - or even a 'Financial Planner', then you could be in trouble. And remember, it can be seen as boring!

But, what if you could communicate your service in an exciting and compelling way? What if you could communicate how your purpose is to tell the *Truth About Money* and to help clients manage their wealth so that it gives them the life they want? Think about it! Why else have wealth if it doesn't give them the life they want? That's a good question, don't you think?

What if you could convey your service in such an inspiring way that clients say *"Wow! That's what I want!!"*

To do this is easier than you think. First, you need to communicate your service in a new way, with the focus OFF investments and instead put firmly on your client.

So, think: how could you adapt your first client meeting (and ongoing client meetings) to bring more of what matters to the fore? How could you differentiate yourself from other Advisers, perhaps using some of the ideas above?

I've shared a few words that I've personally used for many years in this book and you are welcome to give these words a try in your own business.

But, there is one thing I can't share with you in print. It's a powerful client presentation that will enable you to explain your service to your clients AT THE PERFECT TIME and in a compelling way so that clients say ***"Why don't all Financial Advisers do this??!!!"***

If you would like to find out what that presentation is, I'll happily share it with you through the power of video instruction. I'll talk you through it. I'll walk you through it. I'll show you how you can easily adopt it and how it can guarantee your success in the years ahead.

To get access to this proven and effective video instruction, take your next step and sign up for a **no-risk, no obligation 30 day trial** of my **'Seven Step Success System'**.

Sign up here www.FPsuccesssystem.co.uk and over the next few days I'll show you exactly what to say, how to say it and how to absolutely guarantee that you get results.

In fact, if you can't use these ideas to knock your clients socks off, I'll eat my hat and give you my boat :-)

Paul Armson
S/Y Spellbound
Skyros
Greece
January 2016

Update: I've had a number of Advisers ask for some real life examples, so I've popped some case studies at the end of this book. Hope you find them useful.

APPENDIX

Success Habits In Action 1

Case Study No. 1

The Strange Case of 'Mr & Mrs 10 Years Younger'.

I often get asked about actual case studies for Lifestyle Financial Planning. So, in the hope that it might help you to see the immense opportunity for you to make a difference in clients lives, here are a few real life client examples offered by members of Inspiring Advisers. Here, you'll see the Success Habits in action!

Here's the first one. You'll see how a slightly different approach resulted in a client hundreds of times more profitable than most Advisers would have got. Better still, you'll see how this Adviser REALLY matters in the life of this client.

The Strange Case of
'Mr & Mrs Ten Years Younger'

Graham & Pauline were in their late 50's, but looked and felt like they were in their 70's...

They were introduced to our Inspiring Adviser (IA) because they wanted to invest some money into an ISA (a UK tax advantaged savings arrangement). They said they weren't interested in anything else.

But, using various techniques learned from the Inspiring Advisers Coaching Programme, our IA was able to open a more meaningful conversation with Graham & Pauline, (Habit No. 1) and was able to take the focus OFF financial products and instead show genuine interest in Graham & Pauline. (Habit No.2)

He successfully avoided *'The Transaction Trap'!* (Habit No. 4)

It turns out Graham & Pauline were running their own small business and were working 60 – 70 hours a week. In fact,

Sunday mornings were spent finishing off the week's paperwork.

Their small business was slowly killing them!

Holidays? Few and far between.

Hobbies? None.

Stress? Lots.

It's a common problem.

After doing a great first 'discovery' meeting, asking great questions IN THE RIGHT ORDER, all learned from the Inspiring Advisers Online Coaching Programme, and getting to know more about his clients, our IA identified Graham & Pauline's REAL objective....

It wasn't an ISA!

It was to escape from their business and get on with their life!

And Graham's ambition? To learn to fly "*before it's too late*".

But, sadly, their ties and commitment to their business meant this was unlikely to happen.

On talking further with Graham & Pauline it soon became apparent to our IA that over the years substantial funds had been accumulated in various investments including pensions etc. These had been ignored for many years, and because no one had been meddling with their money it had performed quite well.

With further discussion, our IA helped Graham & Pauline identify the cost of their current and future desired lifestyle, including the cost of flying lessons. He needed to understand this in order to calculate their 'Number' – the amount of money they needed for the rest of their life.

In the course of discussions our IA asked about the chances of selling their business.

Amazingly, Graham & Pauline confirmed that an offer had been made within the last 12 months. However, this was turned down on the advice of their accountant. He had advised Graham & Pauline that the £2million offered was under valuing their business and was well below the £4-5 million of potential value that could be realised in the next 5-10 years.

So...!

That's why they were still working!

And that's why their business was slowly killing them!

So, our IA went back to his office, and using leading financial forecasting software, (cashflow modelling) he crunched their Number – the amount of money they needed for the rest of their life.

Here's what he found...

Using PRUDENT assumptions (and after 'stress testing' those assumptions) our IA found that Graham & Pauline needed just an additional £500,000 to retire NOW! (Yes, NOW, not in 3 year's time at aged 60!)

If the cost of flying lessons and the purchase of a light aircraft was built in they needed just £750,000, NOW!

And this was to start living the life they wanted NOW – not in 3, 5 or 10 years time!

Trouble is, they'd just turned down an offer of £2 million!

When Graham & Pauline heard the news they were amazed (Habit 3 - Truth About Money).

With the help of our IA, using cashflow modelling in the Financial Planning meeting, Graham & Pauline began to see what their financial future looked like on prudent assumptions. Our IA demonstrated 'stress testing' the assumptions so Graham & Pauline could feel confident in making decisions moving forward. (Habit No. 5)

Then, with a little help from our IA, Graham then managed to get the deal back on the table and they ended up selling their business for £1.8 million.

So, thanks to our IA, they escaped from their business several years early with complete confidence and certainty over their future.

The stress from their business disappeared. They were free. Their lives were changed.

Graham learned to fly. And both he & Pauline continue to enjoy their retirement.

Better still, they now look – AND FEEL – 10 years younger!

OUTCOMES FOR OUR INSPIRING ADVISER.....

For our IA, because he successfully avoided *'The Transaction Trap'*, and because he asked better questions, he got a lot more than a small investment into an ISA!

Having demonstrated and delivered a high value genuine financial planning service he received FOUR forms of remuneration:

1) Firstly, using a 'Risk Reversal' process he agreed a substantial initial MINIMUM fee for the financial planning strategy - (The Inspiring Advisers Coaching Programme teaches how to do this easily)

2) Secondly, he charged a fee for the recommendation and implementation of a consolidated, low cost, low risk pension and tax efficient investment strategy taking over ALL existing investment assets and ALL proceeds from the sale of their business.

3) He charged an additional fee based on an hourly rate for the 'hand holding advice' provided to Graham and Pauline in the sale of their business.

4) And more important, he continues to receive an annual fee of several thousand pounds EVERY year (equating to

1%pa of their low cost, low risk portfolio of investments) for ongoing 'Lifestyle Financial Planning' advice delivered to Graham & Pauline.

Important Note: His service is NOT based on the managing of Graham & Pauline's' money, but on managing their financial planning strategy. He makes it clear that he does not get paid for trying to deliver exceptional investment returns (there is no need for that) – he gets paid for delivering strategic lifestyle financial planning advice to enable his clients to continue to enjoy their financial independence without fear of ever running out of money.

Using the *'Pro Active' Referral Technique* explained in the Inspiring Advisers Coaching Programme, our Inspiring Adviser has also received numerous referrals from Graham & Pauline to other small business owners needing similar 'exit planning' advice.

This is proof! Clients need to know their Number!

More important, unlike many Financial Advisers, our Inspiring Adviser has a quiet, peaceful life running a highly profitable low risk business that delivers to a limited number of clients a consistent, repeatable, controllable service that is NOT dependent on market returns.

Here's the good news...

There are millions of people trapped in their business, or working in a job they hate, or not living life to the full - because no-one has shown them otherwise.

You can help them. This is YOUR opportunity.

What about you? Would you find this type of approach useful? It's not rocket science. All you need is the right mindset. And the right systems and processes. And this is what I teach. It's all covered by the Inspiring Adviser Seven Step Success System.

To get access to this video instruction, take your next step and sign up for a **no-risk, no obligation 30 day trial** of my **'Seven Step Success System'**. Sign up here www.FPsuccesssystem.co.uk

Success Habits In Action 2

Case Study No. 2

The Case of 'Mr & Mrs Got Too Much'

Here you'll see how a slightly different approach resulted in obtaining a client substantially more profitable than most Advisers would have got. All this because of a 'Lifestyle Financial Planning' approach adopted from the Inspiring Advisers Online Coaching Programme.

John & Mary - The Case of 'Mr & Mrs Got Too Much!'

John & Mary were in their late 60's and happily enjoying their retirement. And so they should!

It was March, the end of the tax year was fast approaching and they were interested in just one thing: using up their annual investment allowance into ISAs (Tax advantaged savings vehicles available in the UK).

So, in a hurry, John was encouraged to meet with our Inspiring Adviser (IA) by one of his golfing pals. John made first contact and was very keen to point out that if they met ALL he wanted to do was sort out his ISA. John said that *"everything else is sorted"*. He just wanted to do his ISA before the end of the tax year!

However, at their first meeting, instead of talking about ISAs, our IA focused on something more important.... John and Mary! (Habit No. 1 & 2)

How?

First, he opened the meeting using a 'proven script' learned from the Inspiring Advisers Online Coaching Programme. This 'script' is a guaranteed way to avoid 'The Transaction Trap'. (Habit 4) It gets clients talking - and NOT about ISAs! It works every time.

Here's what happened....

It turns out John had worked long and hard in a Company that he had helped to grow over many years. He had benefited from his share options. He had accumulated some real wealth.

They had plenty of income in retirement; from his Final Salary pension, from some private pensions, interest off their savings and dividends off their shares and portfolio of ISAs.

They had accumulated some real wealth. And they were enjoying it!

House-wise John & Mary were now 'empty nesters' and were soon to down-scale to a smaller, more manageable property. Their three children had all moved out and their five bedroom house was now too big for them. They had found an apartment overlooking John's Golf Club. Perfect. Their downscale in house value would soon see around £600,000 changing from bricks and mortar into liquid savings.

But what did all this mean? And what about Inheritance Tax?

So, with John & Mary totally engaged in the process - and by asking the RIGHT questions in the RIGHT order - our IA spent some time really getting to know John & Mary, about the life they've had, the life they've got and the life they wanted to continue to enjoy. (Habit 1 & 2) He wanted to understand what John and Mary had planned for their own future, and possibly for their children and grandchildren.

He successfully avoided 'The Transaction Trap' (Habit 4) and COMPLETELY took away the focus of ISAs - or any form of investment. He kept the focus on John and Mary, about what THEY wanted out of life.

Then he helped them to identify the cost of their current lifestyle and the lifestyle they wanted to continue to enjoy – this gave an indication of their 'expenditure' requirements throughout life.

He also reminded them about 'life not being a rehearsal' (Habit 3) and got them to think about what else they might like to do in their lifetime in order to really enjoy their remaining years.

He gathered the facts about what they had accumulated; their capital position, their assets, their liabilities and their many sources of income.

And then, to sum up the meeting, he used the *'Client RWM Presentation'* (which is taught in the Inspiring Advisers

Online Coaching Programme) to explain his service to John & Mary. They were really impressed.

John said: *"Why don't ALL Financial Advisers do this?!"*

Our Inspiring Adviser then returned to his office, and using leading financial forecasting software, (cashflow modelling) together with a thorough understanding of his clients circumstances, and, using 'prudent' assumptions, he 'crunched their Number'. (Habit 5)

This is what he found…

Based on the prudent assumptions they had made, after allowing for inflation, and after allowing for the potential costs of long term nursing care, John & Mary would NEVER run out of money.

In fact, John & Mary's wealth would continue to increase, even after allowing for extra expenditure.

But, John & Mary had a big problem. A different kind of problem to most.

Instead of John & Mary running out of money, John and Mary were well on course to die… with TOO MUCH! (Habit 3 - Truth About Money!)

Why's that a problem?

Here's why…

After having paid tax throughout their whole life, on everything they'd ever earned (income tax and NI), on pretty well everything they'd ever spent (VAT), more tax when John sold his shares (CGT), tax when they each refuel their Mercedes (fuel tax), tax on their wine (alcohol duty) and tax every time they had moved house (Stamp Duty).

In fact, John & Mary were about to pay another slug of tax (£24,000 Stamp Duty) when they soon down-scaled their house.

Tax, tax, *@*@ing tax!

But their biggest tax bill was lurking…

With the help of cashflow modelling software (Habit 5) our Inspiring Adviser helped John & Mary realise the size of their problem, and who was going to be the single, largest beneficiary of John & Mary's hard earned estate…

The Chancellor!

If both John & Mary died now the Inheritance Tax bill would be well over £1.4million. And it was going to get far worse.

But it didn't have to be that way.

So our IA, (using Habit 5 to help John & Mary see what their financial future looked like), helped John & Mary work out just how much more they could afford to spend over the next 10 years while they were still young enough to 'do stuff' - and how much they could confidently afford to pass on to their children NOW and over the next ten years - without fear of them ever running out of money.

Effectively, with the help of his financial planning software, our Inspiring Adviser helped John & Mary confidently create a *'spending & gifting programme'*.

Our IA also helped John & Mary DE-RISK their portfolios! When they realised they didn't want to 'die with TOO MUCH', they understood they could be quite happy with LESS RISK and LESS RETURN - and far MORE peace of mind! (Habit 6)

Result: John & Mary are now on course to completely eliminate their Inheritance Tax liability. They have certainty. They have more peace of mind. They are on course to 'prudently' manage their wealth to give them the life they want whilst gradually passing on wealth down to their children and grandchildren so the Chancellor does not benefit.

They've also booked a 'First Class' Round The World Cruise. And why not?

They can do this, because John & Mary now know – and, more importantly, they understand – their Number.

OUTCOMES FOR OUR INSPIRING ADVISER.....

For our Inspiring Adviser, for a little bit more work they got a lot more than an ISA!

Having demonstrated and delivered a high value genuine financial planning service they received FIVE forms of remuneration:

1) Firstly, using a 'Risk Reversal' process (learned from the Inspiring Adviser Online Coaching Programme) they agreed a substantial initial MINIMUM fee for the financial planning strategy;

2) Second, they charged a fee for the recommendation and implementation of a consolidated, low cost, much reduced

risk investment portfolio for John and Mary including ALL their existing assets, much of which was held with past Advisers and / or stockbrokers.

3) Third, they charged a fee for the recommendation and implementation of a family trust arrangement into which money is transferred annually into a long term strategic investment portfolio for John and Mary's chosen beneficiaries.

4) They charged for the recommendation and implementation of a substantial joint life, second death Estate Protection insurance arrangement to immediately protect their estate.

5) And more important, they continue to receive an annual fee in excess of ten thousand pounds EVERY year (equating to 1%pa of their low cost, low risk total portfolio of investments) for ongoing 'Lifestyle Financial Planning' advice delivered to John and Mary.

Important Note: Their service is NOT based on managing John & Mary's money, but on managing their financial planning strategy, in particular their spending and gifting programme.

They make it clear that, although their service includes monitoring investments and tax efficiently rebalancing their portfolio, they do not get paid for trying to deliver exceptional investment 'returns' (John & Mary don't need that!) – they get paid for delivering strategic comprehensive lifestyle financial planning advice to enable John & Mary to continue to enjoy their financial independence, have total financial peace of mind without the worry of excessive estate taxes on their death.

To date our Inspiring Adviser has saved John & Mary hundreds of thousands in Inheritance Tax. He has also been extremely well paid. Not for saving that tax or managing their investments, but for helping John & Mary (and their family) live a better life - with more confidence, more clarity and less worry.

Our Inspiring Adviser has also received at least two referrals from John & Mary to other golfing pals who were in a similar situation, plus a recommendation from their accountant.

John & Mary continue to be a highly profitable client.

More important, though, unlike many Financial Advisers, our Inspiring Adviser has a quiet, peaceful life running a highly profitable, low risk business that delivers to a limited number of clients a consistent, repeatable, controllable service that is NOT dependent on market returns.

Here's the thing....

Most Advisers would have been 'order takers' and walked away with just an ISA or two. They would have fallen into *The Transaction Trap*. They'd have earned a few quid, but that's about it. Perhaps an investment focused Adviser 'might' have persuaded John & Mary to 'test' them with a little more of their portfolio. But that's all.

A Lifestyle Financial Planning approach, however - delivered PROPERLY - transforms first client meetings and ongoing client relationships, it builds more trust, gets more assets under management, results in much more business and much bigger fees - AND more referrals to the RIGHT type of clients.

Here's your opportunity....

As you can see, this isn't not rocket science. All you need is the right mindset. And the right systems and processes. And this is what I teach. It's all covered by the Inspiring Adviser Seven Step Success System.

To get access to this video instruction, take your next step and sign up for a **no-risk, no obligation 30 day trial** of my **'Seven Step Success System'**. Sign up, (www.FPsuccesssystem.co.uk) and over the next few days I'll show you what to say, how to say it and how to guarantee results.

Success Habits In Action 3

Case Study No. 3

The Case of 'Mr & Mrs Too Much Risk'

Trevor & Sue had recently sold their share of their business having worked hard building it up for 30 years or more.

Aged 60, they had no children whom to pass on their hard earned wealth. And now, like so many people, Trevor's primary concern was *"to ensure a good return on capital"*.

Trevor & Sue had already met with two other financial advisers with a view to investing their money. Each of these advisers had carried out a basic fact find. Then, following regulatory guidelines, they had each put forward their recommendations primarily based on the 'risk profile' they had identified for these clients at their first meeting.

As former business owners, both Trevor & Sue had confirmed to both of these advisers that they were prepared to accept a 'reasonable level of risk' in order to obtain a good return on their hard earned money. Trevor's long held view was that *"in order to accumulate, you have to speculate"*!

So, in order to satisfy Trevor & Sue's requirement for a good return both Advisers had recommended a similar, fairly adventurous investment portfolio which matched their *'average to above average risk profile'* and, they quoted in their suitability reports *"past returns of circa 8% - 10%+ over the long term"* with the usual disclaimers.

Both portfolios suggested a very high proportion of monies to be invested in equities and other volatile investments in an effort to secure a high return over the longer term.

Obviously not totally convinced, Trevor & Sue decided they would invest £100,000 with each Adviser to see how well they did before investing further.

However, before investing their money Trevor & Sue were urged by a friend to speak with our 'Inspiring Adviser' (IA)

Here's what happened...

When our IA met with Trevor & Sue, they did the complete opposite to the other two Advisers. Instead, our IA focused their attention on Trevor & Sue, not their money! (Habit 1 & 2)

Following the methods contained in the Inspiring Advisers Coaching Programme, our IA focused on asking the RIGHT questions, in the RIGHT order.

They first of all focused on getting to really know and understand Trevor & Sue. (Habits 1 & 2) They enquired about the business they had built; when, how and why they started it; the trials and tribulations they had encountered along the way; the successes, the failures; they asked about Trevor & Sue's 'LIFESTYLE'; the sort of things they've enjoyed doing in the past, what they now enjoyed doing - and what sort of things they wanted to do in the future.

Reminding them that 'Life's not a rehearsal' (Habit 3) our IA got to understand their fears and doubts and what was important to them about their future in the time they've got left. (Habit 3)

Through a straightforward process, again adopted from the Inspiring Advisers Coaching Programme, our IA then helped Trevor & Sue identify the cost of their desired lifestyle not only now, but over the various periods of their lives, allowing for inflation and the possible need for long term care. They then helped Trevor & Sue to consider and include into their planning certain additional financial goals and objectives that would make their retirement even more fulfilling and meaningful.

Then our IA returned to their office, and set about producing a meaningful lifestyle financial plan that would give clarity to Trevor & Sue and enable them to make smarter decisions with their money.

With a thorough understanding of their clients, and using leading financial forecasting software (lifelong cash flow modelling), (Habit 5) at the next meeting our IA was then able to graphically demonstrate and prove to Trevor & Sue that on prudent assumptions, in order to prevent ever running out of money, all they needed to achieve was a real rate of return on their money of just 0.5% above inflation.

In other words they didn't need 6%, or 8% or 10% or more a year!

What they needed was prudence, not performance!

With this knowledge, our IA then helped Trevor & Sue understand that having worked so hard over 30 years to accumulate their wealth, the last thing they needed at this stage of their life was risk.

Our IA proved, that what they in fact needed was a **lower return with much less risk**; a prudent, tax efficient portfolio which would give them the peace of mind they needed to enjoy their retirement – without constantly worrying about world stock markets. (Habit 6)

With the economic turmoil of 2008 and more recent volatility of equity and property markets Trevor & Sue were able to avoid the inevitable loss on capital that would have ensued had they invested with the other Advisers without knowing and understanding their full financial situation.

This approach effectively saved Trevor & Sue well over £400,000 of imminent losses that would have occurred had they invested through the other two Advisers who did not do Lifestyle Financial Planning.

Trevor & Sue continue to enjoy their retirement and our IA continues to meet with them on an annual basis to update their financial plan, and, more often than not, discuss how much more they can afford to spend to further enjoy their retirement and continue to be free of worry. (Habit 7)

For Trevor & Sue, their big question was **"Why didn't the other two Advisers do this?"**

OUTCOMES FOR OUR 'INSPIRING ADVISER'.....

First, THEY got ALL Trevor & Sue's business immediately! Not a single penny - went to the other two Advisers.

The 'Lifetime Value' of Trevor & Sue, as a client, is substantial:

Having demonstrated and delivered a high value genuine financial planning service, our IA received THREE forms of remuneration:

1) Firstly, using a client friendly 'Risk Reversal' technique, they agreed a substantial initial MINIMUM fee for the financial planning strategy - but where THEY take the risk, not Trevor & Sue. (I teach this in the Inspiring Advisers Coaching Programme)

2) Secondly, they charged a fee for the recommendation and implementation of a low cost, low risk, tax efficient investment portfolio including the substantial proceeds from the sale of Trevor's business, PLUS the consolidation of all of their pension arrangements.

3) Our Inspiring Adviser continues to receive an annual fee of several thousand pounds EVERY year (equating to 1%pa of their low cost, low risk portfolio of investments) for ongoing 'Lifestyle Financial Planning' advice delivered annually, year after year, to Trevor & Sue via Forward Planning Meetings (Habit 7)

Important Note: Our Inspiring Adviser's service was NOT based on the managing of Trevor & Sue's money, but on managing their financial planning strategy and safeguarding them from unnecessary risk. Our IA made it clear that they do not get paid for trying to deliver performance – they get paid for delivering prudence and strategic lifestyle financial planning advice to enable Trevor & Sue to continue to enjoy their financial independence without fear of ever running out of money - or dying with too much!

Better still, using the techniques I teach in the Inspiring Advisers Coaching Programme our IA also received a number of referrals from Trevor & Sue, including to Trevor's former business partner who then received the SAME service but based on his own personal needs.

More important, unlike most Financial Advisers, this approach has created a quiet, peaceful life for our Inspiring Adviser running a highly profitable, low risk business that delivers to less than 100 clients a consistent, repeatable, controllable service that is NOT dependent on market returns.

Trevor & Sue's question remains a good one. **"Why don't ALL financial advisers work this way?"**

CONSIDER THIS: The other two Advisers had effectively 'stuck pins' in Trevor and Sue (risk profiling) to find out how much pain they can take. They then recommended portfolios that would always deliver that amount of pain. Crazy, eh?

It's ludicrous. And it's happening everywhere.

But here is your opportunity. Just do the opposite to what other Advisers are doing!

This is what delivering Lifestyle Financial Planning is all about.

Here's your opportunity....

It's not rocket science. All you need is the right mindset. And the right systems and processes. And this is what I teach. It's all covered by the Inspiring Adviser Seven Step Success System.

To get access to this video instruction, take your next step and sign up for a **no-risk, no obligation 30 day trial** of my **'Seven Step Success System'**. Sign up, (here: www.FPsuccesssystem.co.uk) and over the next few days I'll show you what to say, how to say it and how to guarantee results in six months or less.

Success Habits In Action 4

Case Study No. 4

This Case Study is Quite Upsetting

This story is really sad. But it might explain my ongoing, often outspoken frustration with the 'Industry' - in particular with Advisers who miss the point altogether and fail to answer their clients BIGGEST questions.

I hate going to funerals. But I'll never forget when I held the hand of Margaret, a newly widowed client. It was a sad moment, when, with tears in our eyes, we both looked down into her husband's grave.

I'd recently witnessed how this lady and her late husband, John, had 'suffered' in the hands of a highly qualified (Chartered and Certified) 'Financial Planner'. A few years earlier this Adviser had happily taken a year's ISA investment off this lovely couple, then in their early sixties. As you'll see, this 'Financial Planner' had failed to identify their REAL needs.

Just before John died, they'd been referred to me by a close friend who was a client of mine. I was told by my client, that they wanted to know, for sure, that Margaret was going to be OK, financially.

At our first meeting they passed me a copy of their Adviser's recommendations from a few years earlier. This Adviser had obviously spent hours researching funds; he'd matched their risk profile perfectly, he'd produced a beautiful Reason Why / Suitability report to document his recommendation - and he'd gone ahead and invested John & Margaret's money into an ISA in a timely fashion. I'd noticed he'd earned about four hundred quid in fees/commission.

"So, where's the problem?" some Advisers might think.

Here's what he DIDN'T do...

Because the Adviser asked the WRONG questions, he did not identify that both John & Margaret were still working in a job they hated.

All the Adviser had done was satisfy his clients' immediate need - for an ISA. So he HADN'T done any PROPER financial planning.

He'd focused on the money, not John & Margaret! So, he didn't ask the right questions, he didn't identify the cost of their current and DESIRED lifestyle, he didn't crunch any numbers, he didn't do a meaningful Lifetime Cashflow.

He didn't identify that, at that time, John & Margaret could have retired immediately and lived happily ever after - without ever running out of money.

John & Margaret were, what I call a *'Just Right'* type of client. They already had enough money for the rest of their life - **but the problem was... they didn't know that!!!!**

Sadly, three years later, John - still stressed and working in a job he hated - found out he'd got a brain tumour and just 6 months to live.

Result: three years of his life had been lost, spent working, in a job he hated - when he could have been playing!

These clients could have easily afforded to retire 5 years earlier!

John could have been spending precious time with Margaret - enjoying what turned out to be only a short amount of time they had left together.

But it's too late.

Instead, John had wasted his precious time working.

Personally, I believe their Adviser had FAILED them. What do you think?

Could John still be alive today had the Adviser removed their stress and worry?

He didn't do any PROPER Financial Planning. (Even though he was parading as a 'Certified' and 'Chartered' Financial Planner - and still does to this day).

Now look. This Adviser was well qualified, well meaning and no doubt a nice guy - but he hadn't done the job properly. He'd focused on the wrong things.

He'd sorted out their ISA - but he hadn't told the 'Truth About Money'. (Habit 3)

And here's the funny thing...

He'd only earned a mere fraction of what he could have earned if only he'd known a better way of doing things.

Question: Using John & Margaret as an example, what value would you place on:

1) Arranging an ISA? (Traditional financial advice)

2) Freeing them from a job they hate and enabling them to have the peace of mind and security that they can enjoy the rest of their lives without fear of ever running out of money, WHATEVER happens? (Lifestyle Financial Planning)

But the Adviser will no doubt say: *"But they only wanted an ISA!" "They didn't want 'financial planning!'"* or the old classic: *"They didn't want to pay a fee!"*

Balderdash, I say! (Or words to that effect!)

Are they a professional, or what?

Are they going to do the job properly, or not?

Are they a PROFESSIONAL Financial Planner - or an order taker?

Or are they just peddling funds on behalf of the investment 'industry'?

If so, they should STOP calling themselves a 'Financial Planner'!

Remember this: the best fund, the best asset allocation, the cheapest product, won't change a client's life.

The Truth About Money will.

Showing clients where they are heading financially, answering their BIG questions - like *'How Much Is Enough?'* - engaging with them about the important things, this is the stuff that clients want – and they'll pay you good money for it!

In fact, isn't it our responsibility to do this?

When you choose to tell clients the 'Truth About Money' - by delivering Lifestyle Financial Planning - there will always be a little bit more work. But, as you should see by now, it's worth it!

Sometimes, it's just a matter of 'Going the Extra Mile' in order to show clients what their financial future really looks like.

Remember, clients won't understand (or pay for) Financial Planning until they EXPERIENCE it. Your job (IF you're a PROPER Financial Planner) is to just do it and let them EXPERIENCE it!

That's when clients take action. And that's when they engage with you and your service. Clients absolutely love it and because of this will happily agree to you being well paid - every year.

Here's your opportunity....

It's not rocket science. All you need is the right mindset. And the right systems and processes. And this is what I teach. It's all covered by the Inspiring Adviser Seven Step Success System.

To get access to this video instruction, take your next step and sign up for a **no-risk, no obligation 30 day trial** of my **'Seven Step Success System'**. Sign up, (at www.FPsuccesssystem.co.uk) and over the next few days I'll show you what to say, how to say it and how to guarantee results within 6 months or less.

Your BIG Opportunity

I hope you've found these case studies useful.

I've got many more examples to show how Lifestyle Financial Planning can make a real difference - and with it, how you can REALLY MATTER in the lives of your clients.

Before I finish, I just want to blow away a few myths.

Reading these case studies it would be easy to think that this approach only works with High Net Worth clients. And it would be easy to get the impression that all my clients were High Net Worth.

They weren't.

Personally, I had a handful of 'wealthy' clients. My biggest client had £3 million investable assets, the next about £2 million, the next about £1.5 and the rest between £250,000 and £1 million. The average was about £400,000.

The majority fell between £250,000 and £600,000 including pensions, investments etc. Some had less than £200,000. One couple had less than £100,000. The latter (less than £100,000) paid a small additional retainer and we had 'Forward Planning meetings bi-annually, and they loved it!

Why am I telling you this?

Two reasons:

1) You don't need 'wealthy' clients to succeed.

2) I didn't always have clients like the ones I've described above!

I accept that over the years I've been more disciplined than most in who I talked to and who I took on as a client (because of the 7 Habits!) But things only started to improve for me when the penny really started to drop about Lifestyle Financial Planning and how my purpose was to tell clients the Truth About Money.

Up until then I'd take on anybody as a client. So I was busy with a lot of 'small' clients, many of whom I couldn't really help; clients who had no control over their future. But, when the penny dropped, things started to change.

Here's what happens....

When you really 'get it'; when the penny really drops; when you really believe in 'The Truth About Money'; when you 'commit'; when you make a stand for PROPER financial planning, THAT is when things change. In fact, that's when your confidence increases and you start turning down more clients than you take on.

And, mysteriously, that's when the Universe says: *"At last! <insert your name here> is serious!" "At last! <Your name> has got it!" "Now, I'll reveal opportunities to help <Your Name> deliver what he / she stands for!"*

And that's when things get weird! YOU start spotting opportunities galore! Opportunities that were always there - but you never saw them! You were probably too busy to even notice!

So, hope you don't mind. I just thought I'd mention this. Don't lose your power by saying *"Well, it's alright for him"* or *"It's easy for him to say so."*

It wasn't always so 'easy'. We must stay away from easy!

All you really need is the right mindset. And the right systems and processes. Oh, and a few good habits.

Remember! This is what I teach! In fact, I get a kick out of helping Advisers 'get it'. It's all covered by the Inspiring Adviser Seven Step Success System. What this means is that you don't have to waste your precious time *'reinventing the wheel'*. Your proven 'short cut to success' as a Lifestyle Financial Planner is ready and waiting for you.

So, here you go... To get access to this inspiring video instruction, take your next step by going here: www.FPsuccesssystem.co.uk

In my time I've met thousands of Advisers, many of whom are stuck in mediocrity because they seem to think they know it all. Many others miss out on golden opportunities because they think they're not good enough or they think they couldn't succeed.

Either way, don't let this happen to you.

Give this a try, because you've got absolutely nothing to lose by doing so. Over to you.

About the Author

Paul Armson has been a Financial Adviser since 1982. He started delivering 'Lifestyle' Financial Planning to WOW his clients in 1990 and built a small but highly profitable fee-based Financial Planning practice, primarily focusing on small business owners and retirees.

For the last seven years, he's been helping other Financial Advisers successfully transition to a highly profitable Lifestyle Financial Planning model. He's well qualified to do so, having delivered this valuable service to clients since the early Nineties, eventually semi-retiring at the age of 45 to start sailing his yacht **Spellbound** around the world.

It was whilst crossing the Atlantic, with a client on board, that his journey into helping other Advisers began. The client, whom Paul had helped to retire years early, asked: *"Why don't all Advisers do what you do? Why don't all Advisers deliver Lifestyle Financial Planning?"*

These simple, but intoxicating questions, helped by the clear ocean air, got Paul thinking! And, returning from his

18 month sailing trip he started helping more Advisers make the most from a Lifestyle Financial Planning approach. He did this through his inspiring workshops, seminars and through one to one coaching.

Paul launched Inspiring Advisers in 2013. It is now a growing community of Lifestyle Financial Planners from the UK and around the globe. Membership includes access to Paul's online coaching programme: *'The Seven Step Success System'* which is a low cost and convenient online coaching system that helps Advisers quickly move to a proper, fee-based financial planning business in order to secure their future in a fee-only transparent commission world.

For your No Risk 30 Day Trial GO HERE: or go to www.FPsuccesssystem.co.uk

Paul is a sought after speaker and speaks regularly in the UK and overseas, he is passionate about changing clients and Advisers lives through the successful delivery of PROPER Financial Planning.

Paul can be contacted at: paul@inspiringadvisers.co.uk

Follow him on Twitter: @InspiredAdviser

Next Steps...

**If you thought this book was useful,
you're really going to love <u>Inspiring Advisers Online
and Paul's 'Seven Step Success System'</u>.**

**You can take your No Risk 30 Day Trial of Inspiring
Advisers and benefit from the 'Seven Step Success
System' by going here.**

Or go to www.FPsuccesssystem.co.uk

**But be prepared.... for a lot more pleasure
and a lot less pain!**

---

www.FPsuccesssystem.co.uk